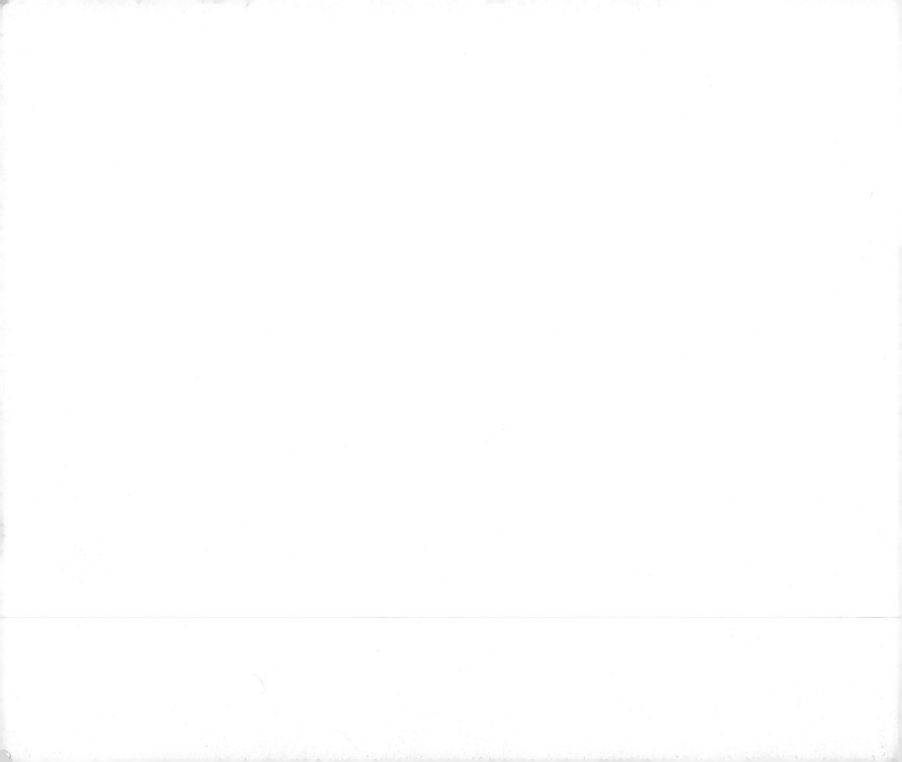

Missing Mittens

by Stuart J. Murphy

illustrated by G. Brian Karas

HarperCollins Publishers

To Blitzen—who could use two pairs of mittens.
He needs an even four.
—S. J. M.

For the Chancellor Livingston Library
—G. B. K.

The publisher and author would like to thank Patricia Chase, Phyllis Goldman,
and Patrick Hopfensperger for their help in making the math in MathStart just right for kids.

HarperCollins®, 🏢®, and MathStart® are registered trademarks of HarperCollins Publishers.
For more information about the MathStart series, write to HarperCollins Children's Books,
1350 Avenue of the Americas, New York, NY 10019, or visit our website at www.mathstartbooks.com.

Bugs incorporated in the MathStart series design were painted by Jon Buller.

Missing Mittens
Text copyright © 2001 by Stuart J. Murphy
Illustrations copyright © 2001 by G. Brian Karas

Library of Congress Cataloging-in-Publication Data
Murphy, Stuart J., 1942–
    Mising Mittens / by Stuart J. Murphy ; illustrated by G. Brian Karas.
        p.   cm. — (MathStart)
    "Level 1, Odd and even numbers."
    Summary: As a farmer tries to find the correct number of mittens for his various farmyard animals, the
reader is introduced to odd and even numbers.
    ISBN 0-06-028026-3. — ISBN 0-06-028027-1 (lib. bdg.). — ISBN 0-06-446733-3 (pbk.)
    1. Counting—Juvenile literature.   2. Numbers—Natural—Juvenile literature.   [1. Numbers, Natural.
2. Counting.]   I. Karas, G. Brian, ill.   II. Title.   III. Series.
QA113.M87 2001   99-41334
513.2'11—dc21   CIP
                                                                                                                         AC

Typography by Elynn Cohen
3 4 5 6 7 8 9 10
❖
First Edition

Missing Mittens

Farmer Bill was shivering.
Snow was in the air.
He looked out on the stormy day
and wondered what to wear.

"Long underwear!" said Bill.
"And my brand-new coat. I'll get
my hat and scarf and earmuffs.
But I'm not ready yet."

"Where are my two mittens?"
Only one was there.
Just one odd mitten by itself—
One mitten's not a pair.

ONE 1

Odd

TWO 2

Even

Bill went out to milk his cow,
as cold as she could be.
They looked for her four mittens,
but there were only three.

Only three odd mittens—
they couldn't find one more.
Any cow needs more than three;
she needs an even four.

Next were his three chickens.
They were huddled in their pen.
They wished they had six mittens—
two mittens for each hen.

Bill looked and found five mittens,
but they really needed six.
Without an even number,
one hen was in a fix.

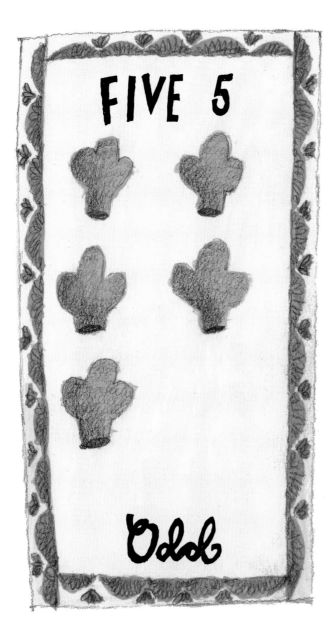

FIVE 5

Odd

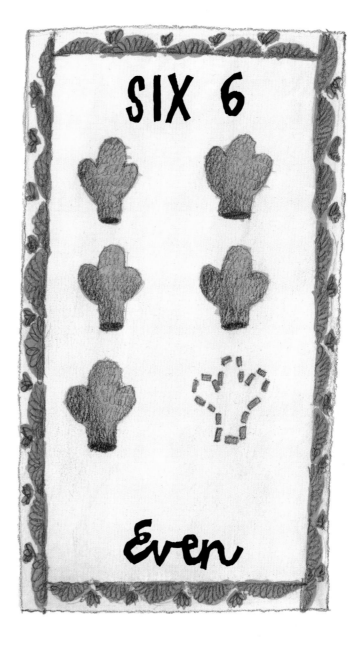

SIX 6

Even

Bill went to see the horses.
Both were shaking in their stall.
Each needed four warm mittens—
that's eight mittens in all.

But there were only seven.
One horse would catch a chill.
Seven mittens for eight hooves—
"How very odd!" said Bill.

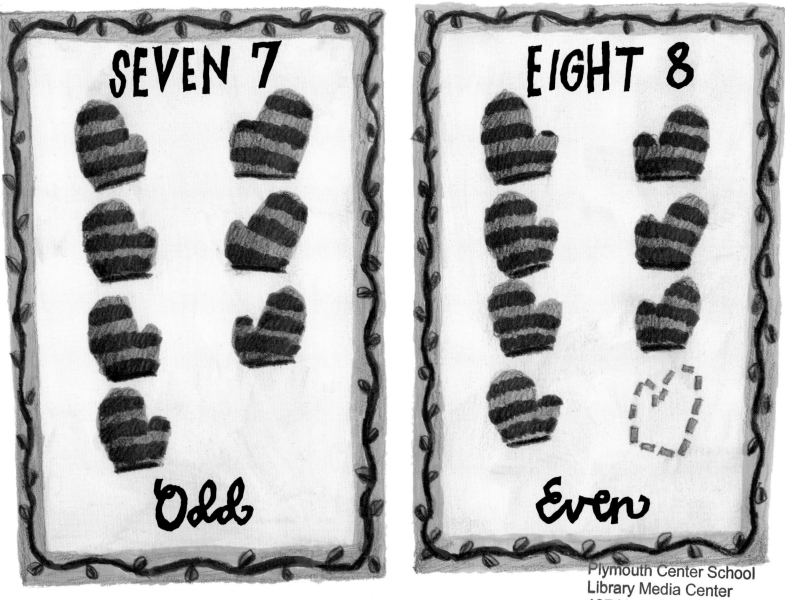

Where were the missing mittens?
How could they be found?
"A mitten thief has been here!"
Bill scratched his head and frowned.

"We must get back our mittens!
Hey, what is that goat doing?
This is no time for breakfast
but it looks like he is . . .

CHEWING!"

Now every hand and foot and hoof
was snug and toasty warm.
And everything was fine again—

until the next big storm.

30

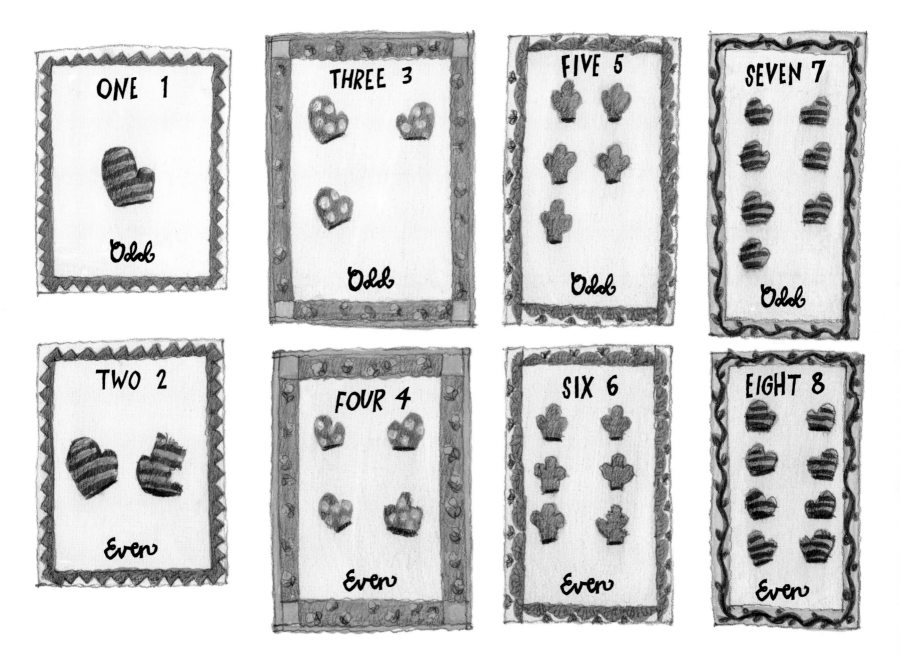

ONE 1
Odd

TWO 2
Even

THREE 3
Odd

FOUR 4
Even

FIVE 5
Odd

SIX 6
Even

SEVEN 7
Odd

EIGHT 8
Even

In *Missing Mittens*, the math concept is even and odd numbers. Identifying even and odd numbers is important to understanding our number system. It will help prepare children to group whole number operations.

If you would like to have more fun with the math concepts presented in *Missing Mittens*, here are a few suggestions:

- Read the story with the child and describe what is going on in each picture. After page 19 ask the child to predict what will happen next in the story. After page 25 ask the child to guess where the missing mittens are.

- Help the child understand the difference between an even and odd number. Draw a line down the center of a piece of paper. On one side represent some even numbers by drawing pairs of small objects. On the other side, show odd numbers by drawing pairs of objects plus one more. Have the child tell you how the even numbers are alike and how the odd numbers are alike.

- Reread the story together and count the number of mittens in each picture. Point out that the animals need one more mitten than is present. Talk about why the animals need an even number of mittens, and why they always have an odd number.

- Ask the child how many mittens would be needed for two dogs. Five cats? The child's whole family?

Following are some activities that will help you extend the concepts presented in *Missing Mittens* into a child's everyday life.

Shopping: While shopping in the supermarket, help your child find objects that come packaged in even numbers or odd numbers.

Playing Games: The first player rolls two dice and figures out if the numbers are even or odd. If both numbers are even (or odd), the first player wins a point. If one is even and the other is odd, the second player wins a point. Then the second player rolls the dice. The first player to win 15 points wins the game.

Button Fun: Place a small pile of buttons on a table. Is there an even number or an odd number of buttons in the pile? Place a second pile on the table. Is there an even number or an odd number of buttons in that pile? Add them together. Is that number even or odd? Make new piles and try the activity many times. Do you get an even or an odd number when you add two evens together? Two odds? An odd and an even?

The following stories include concepts similar to those that are presented in *Missing Mittens*:

- THE CRAYON COUNTING BOOK by Pam Muñoz Ryan and Jerry Pallotta
- EVEN STEVEN AND ODD TODD by Kathryn Cristaldi
- 12 WAYS TO GET TO 11 by Eve Merriam